Tom and Kate Choose Green Carbon

CHILDREN SAVING OUR PLANET SERIES

CAROL SUTTERS

Illustrated by William Fong

AuthorHouse™ UK
1663 Liberty Drive
Bloomington, IN 47403 USA
www.authorhouse.co.uk
UK TFN: 0800 0148641 (Toll Free inside the UK)
UK Local: 02036 956322 (+44 20 3695 6322 from outside the UK)

Because of the dynamic nature of the Internet, any web addresses or links contained in this book may have changed since publication and may no longer be valid. The views expressed in this work are solely those of the author and do not necessarily reflect the views of the publisher, and the publisher hereby disclaims any responsibility for them.

Any people depicted in stock imagery provided by Getty Images are models, and such images are being used for illustrative purposes only.
Certain stock imagery © Getty Images.

This book is printed on acid-free paper.

ISBN: 978-1-6655-8616-0 (sc)
ISBN: 978-1-6655-8617-7 (e)

Library of Congress Control Number: 2021903234

Print information available on the last page.

Published by AuthorHouse 03/31/2021

authorHOUSE®

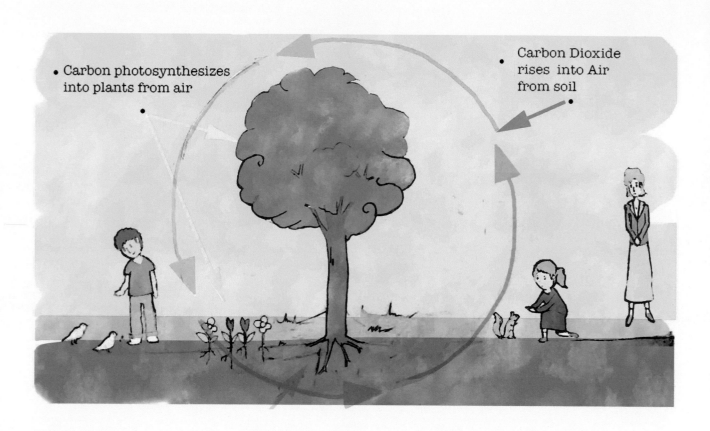

- Carbon photosynthesizes into plants from air

- Carbon Dioxide rises into Air from soil

Green carbon is the carbon in living things. The carbon cycle is in the sea, the air and the soil and it is the carbon of living things and it is already part of the climate.

"What are forms of green carbon?", asks Kate.

Mum replies, "If we plant a tree and grow it in our garden then we cut the wood and burn it in our fire this is green carbon. This is part of the normal carbon cycle. Green carbon is the carbon found in plants and natural living systems and it is part of the carbon cycle."

"Coal is dug out from coal mines below the earth's surface and burnt to generate heat and energy."

"But burning it in large quantities produces too much carbon dioxide which causes pollution. In the past, ships and trains were powered by coal."

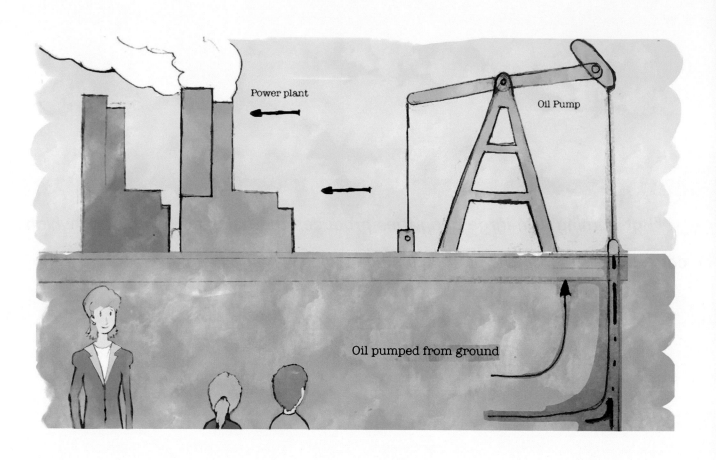

Power plant

Oil Pump

Oil pumped from ground

"Oil is pumped out from below the ground and has many uses. Oil can also be burned for heat, but it is also broken down in oil refineries into many other things."

"Oil can be used to make petrol, gasoline, paraffin, and all sorts of different plastics. Carrier bags made out of plants are a source of green carbon compared to a plastic bag which is made from petrol, a fossil fuel."

"We can adapt our car to use more alcohol fuel mixed with petrol and so use less fossil fuel. This alcohol is bioethanol, a renewable fuel made from growing and fermenting crops like sugar, wheat and maize. Electric battery cars are also being introduced and we are trying to replace coal power stations that generate electricity." Mum continues, "In the future, fighter jets will use biofuels made from algae and household waste, to reduce use of fossil fuels."

"The problem arises if we burn too much fossil fuel and if we make too many plastics. Too much carbon dioxide causes the temperature to rise above normal and affects living plants and animals and it is changing the climate."

"Plastic does not decompose so needs to be burnt releasing more toxic gases for plants and animals. Also plastic causes pollution in seas and on land and it is harmful to many creatures. It breaks down into tiny microplastics. We are trying to reduce our use of plastics."

That summer the family decided to go to visit the grandparents at the seaside travelling by an electric train and not by plane. The aeroplane would have used fossil fuel for energy to enable it to fly. However the train was powered by electricity which had been generated by wind and sea wave power.

What did we learn today? (tick the box if you understood and agree)

☐ Carbon is called either green carbon or fossil carbon.

☐ Green carbon is carbon that comes from the normal carbon cycle and it is safe to use.

☐ Fossil carbon comes from the decomposition of plants and animals that lived many thousands of years ago and it when it burns it harms our world as it produces excess carbon in the air.

☐ Fossil fuels like oil have been very useful to us in enabling us to make plastics, but plastics are difficult to destroy and can cause harm.

Find out about Trees and Deforestation in book 4.

Children Saving our Planet Series

Books

1. **Tom and Kate Go to Westminster CHILDREN'S REVOLT**

2. **Kate and Tom Learn About Fossil Fuels**

3. **Tom and Kate Chose Green Carbon**

4. **Tress and Deforestation**

5. **Our Neighbourhood Houses**

6. **Our Neighbourhood Roads**

7. **Shopping at the Farm Shop**

8. **Travelling to a Holiday by the Sea**

9. **Picnic at the Seaside on Holiday**

These series of simple books explain the landmark importance of Children's participation in the Extinction rebellion protest. Children actively want to encourage and support adults to urgently tackle both the Climate and the Biodiversity emergencies. The booklets enable children at an early age to understand some of the scientific principles that are affecting the destruction of the planet. If global political and economic systems fail to address the climate emergency, the responsibility will rest upon children to save the Planet for themselves.

This series is dedicated to

Theodore, Aria and Ophelia.

Printed in the United States
by Baker & Taylor Publisher Services